cookies

cookies

RYLAND
PETERS
& SMALL

LONDON NEW YORK

Designer Sally Powell

Commissioning Editor
Julia Charles

Picture Research
Emily Westlake

Production Eleanor Cant

Art Director Anne-Marie Bulat

Publishing Director
Alison Starling

Index Hilary Bird

Notes
All spoon measurements
are level unless otherwise
specified. If you are using
a fan-assisted oven, adjust
cooking times according to
manufacturer's instructions.

First published in Great
Britain in 2006
by Ryland Peters & Small
20–21 Jockey's Fields
London WC1R 4BW
www.rylandpeters.com

10 9 8 7 6 5 4 3 2 1

Text copyright © Linda
Collister, Clare Ferguson,
Liz Franklin, Louise Pickford,
Fran Warde, Ryland Peters &
Small 2006

Design and photographs
copyright ©
Ryland Peters & Small 2006

ISBN-13: 978 1 84597 290 5
ISBN-10: 1 84597 290 2

A CIP catalogue record for this
book is available from the
British Library.

Printed in China

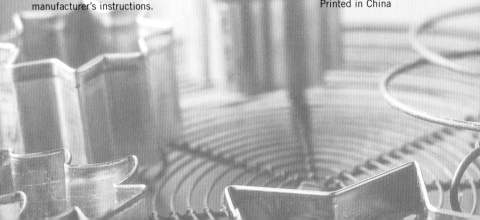

contents

introduction

Who can resist a homemade cookie still warm from the oven? Add a good cup of coffee, tea or glass of chilled milk and settle down to enjoy a moment of pure pleasure. Here you will find the perfect cookie recipe for every occasion. Whether you want to enjoy a little luxury every day, spoil yourself with an occasional self-indulgent treat or surprise a friend with a thoughtful gift, these simple, no-fuss recipes make it easy. You will need to use the very best ingredients to get the best cookies so buy the highest quality you can find and you'll really appreciate the results. But be warned, you may never want to eat a shop-bought cookie again once you've baked your own!

cookie jar classics

These cookies are always popular, whether plain or flavoured with dried fruit. Use old-fashioned porridge oats or rolled oats rather than the 'instant' variety.

classic oat cookies

115 g unsalted butter, very soft

140 g light muscovado sugar

1 large egg, beaten

1 tablespoon whole milk

½ teaspoon real vanilla essence

100 g self-raising flour

75 g dried fruit (raisins, cherries, cranberries or blueberries)

150 g porridge oats

several baking trays, very lightly greased

makes about 24

Put the butter, sugar, egg, milk and vanilla in a bowl and beat well using an electric mixer or whisk, or a wooden spoon. Add the flour, dried fruit and porridge oats and mix well with the wooden spoon.

Put heaped teaspoons of dough onto the prepared baking trays, spacing them well apart.

Bake in a preheated oven at 180°C (350°F) Gas 4 for 12–15 minutes until lightly browned around the edges.

Let cool on the trays for 2 minutes, then transfer to a wire rack to cool completely.

Store in an airtight container and eat within 5 days or freeze for up to a month.

For the best flavour, use a good-quality peanut butter with no added sugar. The crunchy coating is made by rolling the cookie mixture in roasted (but unsalted) peanuts before baking.

extra-crunchy peanut butter cookies

115 g unsalted butter, softened

125 g crunchy peanut butter

140 g light muscovado sugar

1 large egg, lightly beaten

½ teaspoon real vanilla essence

225 g self-raising flour

200 g roasted unsalted peanut halves

several baking trays, greased

makes about 20

Put the soft butter, peanut butter, sugar, beaten egg, vanilla and flour in a large bowl. Mix well with a wooden spoon.

When thoroughly combined, take walnut-sized portions of the dough (about a tablespoon) and roll into balls with your hands. Put the peanut halves in a shallow dish, then roll the dough in the nuts. Arrange the balls well apart on the prepared trays, then gently flatten slightly with your fingers.

Bake in a preheated oven at 180°C (350°F) Gas 4 for 12–15 minutes until light golden brown.

Let cool on the trays for a couple of minutes to firm up, then transfer to a wire rack to cool completely.

Store in an airtight container and eat within 5 days or freeze for up to a month.

For a spicier Stem Ginger Cookie simply replace the treacle with golden syrup and add 40 g of finely chopped preserved ginger along with the egg.

gingerbread cookies

350 g self-raising flour

a pinch of salt

200 g golden caster sugar, plus extra for sprinkling

2 teaspoons ground ginger

2 teaspoons ground cinnamon

1 teaspoon bicarbonate of soda

115 g unsalted butter

85 g black treacle

1 large egg, beaten

several baking trays, lightly greased

makes about 30

Sift the flour, salt, sugar, ginger, cinnamon and bicarbonate of soda into a large bowl. Heat the butter and black treacle very gently in a small saucepan until melted. Pour onto the dry ingredients, add the beaten egg and mix thoroughly with a wooden spoon.

Using your hands, roll the dough into 30 walnut-sized balls. Arrange well apart on the prepared trays, then flatten with your fingers. Sprinkle with a little sugar, then bake in a preheated oven at 160°C (325°F) Gas 3 for 12–15 minutes or until firm and lightly browned.

Remove from the oven and let cool on the trays for 2 minutes. Transfer to a wire rack to cool completely.

Store in an airtight container and eat within 5 days or freeze for up to a month.

Walnuts make wonderful biscuits, but other nuts such as pecans or hazelnuts will also work just as well in this recipe.

walnut cookies

90 g unsalted butter, at room temperature

80 g golden caster sugar

80 g unrefined demerara sugar

1 large egg, beaten

½ teaspoon real vanilla essence

250 g self-raising flour

70 g walnut pieces, chopped

several baking trays, lightly greased

makes about 24

Using a wooden spoon or electric mixer, beat the butter until soft and creamy. Gradually beat in the sugars and continue beating for another 2 minutes.

Beat in the egg a little at a time, then stir in the vanilla essence, flour and nuts. Work the mixture with your hands until it comes together into a firm dough. Again using your hands, roll the dough into 24 walnut-sized balls.

Put the balls, spaced well apart, on the baking trays, then flatten with a fork. Bake in a preheated oven at 180°C (350°F) Gas 4 for about 10 minutes, until golden and firm.

Remove from the oven, leave on the baking trays for a couple of minutes to firm up, then transfer to a wire rack to cool completely.

Store in an airtight container and eat within 1 week, or freeze for up to a month.

Always popular and hard to beat! This classic recipe has been adapted so that it uses less sugar and more nuts. Use plain chocolate broken up into chunks or a bag of good quality chocolate chips.

classic choc chip cookies

175 g self-raising flour

a pinch of salt

a good pinch of bicarbonate of soda

115 g unsalted butter, very soft

60 g caster sugar

60 g light muscovado sugar

½ teaspoon real vanilla essence

1 large egg, lightly beaten

175 g plain chocolate broken into chunks or chocolate chips

75 g walnut or pecan pieces

several baking trays, lightly greased

makes about 24

Put all the ingredients in a large bowl and mix thoroughly with a wooden spoon.

Drop heaped teaspoons of the mixture onto the prepared trays, spacing them well apart.

Bake in a preheated oven at 190°C (375°F) Gas 5 for 8–10 minutes until lightly coloured and just firm.

Let cool on the trays for a minute, then transfer to a wire rack to cool completely.

Store in an airtight container and eat within 5 days or freeze for up to a month.

Parkin is a kind of sticky gingerbread from Yorkshire, made with oatmeal, black treacle and spice. These cookies are made from the same ingredients and have the same flavour and a crunchy texture.

parkin cookies

115 g self-raising flour

115 g fine oatmeal

1 teaspoon ground ginger

½ teaspoon ground allspice

3 tablespoons dark muscovado sugar

85 g unsalted butter

2 tablespoons golden syrup

1 tablespoon black treacle

icing sugar, for dusting (optional)

several baking trays, lightly greased

makes about 20

Put the flour, oatmeal, ginger, allspice and sugar in a large bowl and mix well. Make a hollow in the centre.

Put the butter, golden syrup and treacle in a small saucepan and heat gently until melted. Pour the mixture into the hollow in the dry ingredients and mix well with a wooden spoon.

Using floured hands, take walnut-sized portions of the dough (about a tablespoon) and roll into balls. Set well apart on the prepared trays. Bake in a preheated oven at 180°C (350°F) Gas 4 for 15 minutes until firm.

Let cool on the trays for 2 minutes to firm up, then transfer to a wire rack to cool completely. Serve dusted with icing sugar, if using.

Store in an airtight container and eat within 5 days or freeze for up to a month.

heavenly chocolate

Make chocolate chips by chopping a bar of good plain chocolate into large chunks – the flavour is far superior to commercial chocolate chips.

black and white cookies

115 g unsalted butter, at room temperature

85 g light brown muscovado sugar

1 large egg, beaten

60 g self-raising flour

½ teaspoon baking powder

a pinch of salt

½ teaspoon real vanilla essence

115 g porridge oats (not instant)

175 g plain chocolate, chopped into chunks

several baking trays, lightly greased

makes about 24

Using a wooden spoon or electric mixer, beat the butter until creamy. Add the sugar and beat until light and fluffy. Gradually beat in the egg, beating well after the last addition. Sift the flour, baking powder and salt into the mixture, add the vanilla essence and oats and stir in. When thoroughly mixed, stir in the chocolate chunks.

Put heaped teaspoons of the cookie mixture, spaced well apart, on the prepared trays. Bake in a preheated oven at 180°C (350°F) Gas 4 for 12–15 minutes until golden and just firm. Remove from the oven and let cool on the trays for a couple of minutes until firm enough to transfer to a wire rack to cool completely.

Store in an airtight container. Eat within 1 week, or freeze for up to a month.

Good quality plain chocolate is mixed into these cookies as chunks and as a powder (by simply processing it with the flour).

double chocolate pecans

100 g porridge oats or rolled oats (not instant)

140 g plain flour

½ teaspoon baking powder

½ teaspoon bicarbonate of soda

85 g light muscovado sugar

200 g plain chocolate, broken up

115 g unsalted butter, very soft

1 large egg, beaten

100 g pecan pieces

several baking trays, lightly greased

makes about 24

Put the oats in a food processor. Add the flour, baking powder, bicarbonate of soda, the sugar and half of the chocolate pieces. Process until the mixture has a sandy texture.

Put the soft butter, beaten egg, pecan pieces and the remaining pieces of chocolate in a large bowl. Add the mixture from the processor and mix well with a wooden spoon or your hands to make a firm dough.

Roll walnut-sized pieces of dough into balls using your hands. Arrange well apart on the prepared baking trays and flatten slightly with the back of a fork. Bake in a preheated oven at 190°C (375°F) Gas 5 for 12–15 minutes until almost firm.

Let cool on the trays for 2 minutes, then transfer to a wire rack to cool completely.

Store in an airtight container and eat within 5 days or freeze for up to a month.

A very quick, rich recipe using plain chocolate and a food processor. These cookies are particularly good served with vanilla ice cream.

chocolate fudge cookies

75 g caster sugar

75 g light muscovado sugar

140 g good plain chocolate, broken up

110 g unsalted butter, chilled and diced

150 g plain flour

½ teaspoon baking powder

1 large egg, lightly beaten

several baking trays, greased

makes about 20

Put both the caster and muscovado sugars in a food processor. Add the pieces of chocolate, then process until the mixture has a sand-like texture.

Add the pieces of butter, flour, baking powder and egg and process until the mixture comes together to make a firm dough. Carefully remove from the machine.

Lightly flour your hands and roll the dough into about 20 walnut-sized balls. Arrange them, spaced well apart, on the prepared trays. Bake in a preheated oven at 180°C (350°F) Gas 4 for 12–15 minutes until firm.

Let cool on the trays for 2 minutes, then transfer to wire racks to cool completely.

Store in an airtight container and eat within 5 days or freeze for up to a month.

These dark, dark chocolate cookies have a white 'crazy-paving' top. The effect is created by rolling the cookies in icing sugar just before baking. The surface then cracks to form the 'paving'.

chocolate crackle cookies

100 g plain chocolate, broken up

115 g unsalted butter, diced

175 g light muscovado sugar

1 large egg, beaten

2–3 drops real vanilla essence

175 g self-raising flour

½ teaspoon bicarbonate of soda

2 tablespoons icing sugar

several baking trays, greased

makes about 24

Put the chocolate, butter and sugar in a heatproof bowl and set over a saucepan of gently steaming water. Melt gently, stirring occasionally until smooth.

Remove the bowl from the pan and let cool for a minute. Stir in the egg, vanilla, flour and bicarbonate of soda. Mix well. Cover the bowl and chill until firm, about 20 minutes.

Put the icing sugar in a shallow dish. Using your hands, roll the dough into walnut-sized balls, then roll in the icing sugar to coat thoroughly. Set the balls on the prepared trays, spacing them well apart. Bake in a preheated oven at 200°C (400°F) Gas 6 for 10–12 minutes until just set.

Let cool on the tray for 2 minutes, then transfer to a wire rack to cool completely.

Store in an airtight container and eat within 5 days or freeze for up to a month.

Only the very finest chocolate is suitable for this sophisticated cookie, preferably with at least 70 per cent cocoa solids and very little sugar.

bitter chocolate butter cookies

70 g plain chocolate, roughly chopped

35 g golden caster sugar

220 g unsalted butter, chilled and diced

140 g light brown muscovado sugar

250 g plain flour

½ teaspoon real vanilla essence

50 g white or plain chocolate, melted, to finish

several baking trays, well greased

makes about 30

Put the chopped chocolate and caster sugar in a food processor and process until they form the texture of sand. Add the diced butter, sugar, flour and vanilla essence, then process again just until the dough comes together.

Using your hands, form the dough into about 30 walnut-sized balls. Arrange them on the prepared baking trays, spacing them well apart.

Bake the biscuits in a preheated oven at 180°C (350°F) Gas 4 for 10–15 minutes or until they are just firm to the touch and beginning to colour around the edges.

Remove from the oven. Leave them for 5 minutes to firm up before transferring to a wire rack to cool. When they are cold, decorate by drizzling with the melted chocolate.

Store in an airtight container and eat within 4 days. Undecorated biscuits can be frozen for up to a month.

These delicious macaroons have a crisp outside and are soft and chewy inside but it is the creamy white chocolate filling that makes them extra special.

double chocolate macaroons

75 g plain chocolate, chopped

2 large egg whites, at room temperature

200 g caster sugar

125 g ground almonds

2–3 drops almond essence

110 g white chocolate, chopped

100 ml double cream

several baking trays, lined with non-stick baking parchment

makes about 8

Put the plain chocolate into a heatproof bowl set over a pan of steaming water and melt gently. Remove the bowl from the heat and stir until smooth. Set aside. Put the egg whites into a bowl and whisk until stiff peaks form. Gradually whisk in the sugar to make a thick, glossy meringue. Fold in the almonds, almond essence and melted chocolate. When blended, put a tablespoonful of the mixture at a time onto the baking trays and spread to discs about 5 cm across.

Bake in a preheated oven at 150°C (300°F) Gas 2 for 30 minutes until just firm. Remove from the oven and let cool on the trays. When cold, gently peel away from the paper.

Put the white chocolate and cream into a small saucepan and heat very gently, until melted and smooth. Remove from the heat, let cool, then beat until thick and fluffy. Use it to sandwich the cold macaroons together.

Store in an airtight container. Best eaten within 5 days.

A few drops of Tabasco sauce gives these moist and rich cookies a fascinating, subtle flavour. Ask your friends if they can guess the mystery ingredient!

macadamia and white choc chilli cookies

150 g macadamia nuts

200 g plain flour

½ teaspoon baking powder

100 g light muscovado sugar

115 g unsalted butter, very soft

1 large egg, lightly beaten

5 drops Tabasco sauce

100 g white chocolate, broken into chunks

several baking trays, lightly greased

makes about 20

Put the nuts in an ovenproof dish and toast in a preheated oven at 180°C (350°F) Gas 4 for 5–7 minutes until light golden brown. Let cool, then chop coarsely by hand or in a food processor. Leave the oven on.

Put the chopped nuts, flour, baking powder, sugar, butter, egg, Tabasco and chocolate pieces in a large bowl and mix thoroughly with a wooden spoon.

Using about a tablespoon of the mixture for each cookie, drop each spoonful onto the prepared baking trays, spacing well apart. Bake in the heated oven for 12–15 minutes until light golden brown.

Let cool on the trays for 2 minutes, then transfer to a wire rack to cool completely.

Store in an airtight container and eat within 4 days or freeze for up to a month.

occasional treats

Pecans are the most popular nuts in North America, and were particularly prized by Algonquin Indians, who gave them their name paccan. In the South, they are used to enrich stuffings, breads, cakes and cookies, as well as baked in pies. These rich and crumbly cookies are found in New Mexico.

santa fe wedding cookies

130 g plain flour

4 tablespoons light muscovado sugar

100 g unsalted butter, very soft

½ teaspoon real vanilla essence

50 g pecan pieces, coarsely chopped

20 pecan halves, to decorate

icing sugar, to dust

several baking trays, greased

makes about 20

Put the flour, sugar, soft butter, vanilla and pecans in a bowl. Using a wooden spoon, work the ingredients until they come together to form a soft dough.

Using your hands, lightly floured, roll the mixture into about 20 walnut-sized balls. Arrange them slightly apart on the prepared baking trays, then gently press a pecan half on top of each cookie. Bake in a preheated oven at 180°C (350°F) Gas 4 for 10–12 minutes until a light golden colour with slightly brown edges.

Remove from the oven, let cool on the trays for 2 minutes, then transfer to a wire rack to cool completely. Dust with plenty of icing sugar before serving. Handle carefully as these cookies are fragile.

Store in an airtight container and eat within 5 days, or freeze for up to a month.

These sweet, almond-rich cookies are like soft, chewy amaretti. Serve with coffee at the end a special meal or give a box of them as a gift.

sardinian wedding cookies

450 g almond paste

70 g flaked almonds

2 medium egg whites

50 g icing sugar

30 g flaked almonds

several baking trays, lined with non-stick baking parchment

makes about 30

Break up the almond paste and put in a food processor. Process briefly until the paste is finely chopped. Add the almonds, egg whites and sugar and process until the mixture forms a thick, smooth paste.

Using a tablespoon of mixture for each cookie, drop or spoon the mixture onto the prepared trays, spacing the cookies slightly apart. Scatter the remaining almonds over the top of the cookies.

Bake in a preheated oven at 150°C (300°F) Gas 2 for about 25 minutes until light golden brown. Let cool completely on the trays, then remove the cookies.

Store in an airtight container and eat within a week. These cookies don't freeze very well.

These cookies are made with the same ingredients used for a traditional British Christmas cake. Use mixed dried fruit or the 'luxury' type, which includes cherries, and a mix of nuts such as Brazils, walnuts, almonds and hazelnuts.

christmas cake cookies

225 g self-raising flour

⅛ teaspoon grated nutmeg

½ teaspoon mixed spice

110 g dark muscovado sugar

110 g unsalted butter, chilled and diced

2 large eggs, beaten

2 tablespoons sweet sherry, brandy or milk

100 g chopped mixed nuts

150 g mixed dried fruit

Demerara sugar, for sprinkling

several baking trays, greased

makes about 20

Sieve the flour, nutmeg and mixed spice into a large bowl. Stir in the sugar. Add the pieces of butter and rub into the flour using the tips of your fingers until the mixture looks like coarse crumbs. You can also cut the butter into the flour using a knife or special pastry cutter. Add the eggs, sherry, brandy or milk, nuts and dried fruit to the bowl and mix thoroughly with a wooden spoon.

Drop tablespoons of the mixture onto the prepared trays, spacing them well apart. Flatten them slightly with the back of a fork and sprinkle lightly with Demerara sugar.

Bake in a preheated oven at 180°C (350°F) Gas 4 for 12–15 minutes, until golden brown. Let cool on the trays for 2 minutes to firm up, then transfer to a cooling rack to cool completely.

Store in an airtight container and eat within 5 days, or freeze for up to a month.

These fragrant, crumbly *kourambiedes* are served all year round, but especially at Christmas, usually with syrupy fruit and nut preserves, known as *glyka*.

greek shortbread cookies

425 g butter, softened

115 g caster sugar

2 egg yolks

1 teaspoon real vanilla essence

2 tablespoons Greek Metaxa brandy or Cognac

20 green cardamom pods, crushed, black seeds extracted

50 g flaked almonds, chopped or crushed

1 teaspoon baking powder

500–550 g plain flour, sifted

To finish:

2 tablespoons Greek Metaxa brandy or Cognac

2 tablespoons rosewater

150 g icing sugar, sifted

several baking trays, greased

makes about 34

Put the butter and sugar in a bowl and beat until light and pale. Beat in the egg yolks, vanilla, brandy, cardamom and almonds. Add the baking powder and two-thirds of the flour and stir to form a soft, sticky dough. Stir in enough of the remaining flour to make a soft, manageable dough.

Take 1 heaped tablespoon of dough, put it on a floured work surface and roll it into an oval. Set it on one of the prepared baking trays, then push and pinch the ends into a half-moon shape. Repeat this process to make 34 pieces.

Bake in a preheated oven at 160°C (325°F) Gas 3 for 20–22 minutes or until pale, golden and firm, then remove and let cool on wire racks.

Mix the rosewater and brandy in a bowl. Put the icing sugar in another. Partially dip each cookie in the flavouring, then dip it into the sifted icing sugar until thickly coated. Lift out.

Store in layers in a greaseproof paper lined container until ready to serve. Best eaten within 5 days.

These cookies can be made into pretty Christmas decorations by cutting the dough into tree, star or bell shapes and threading with ribbons for hanging.

german honey spice cookies

150 g plain flour

1 teaspoon ground cinnamon

¼ teaspoon ground ginger

¼ teaspoon ground mixed spice

85 g unsalted butter, chilled and diced

3 tablespoons clear honey

To finish (optional):

thin ribbon for hanging, edible icing writing pens, silver balls

shaped cookie cutters

several baking trays, greased

makes about 12

Put the flour, cinnamon, ginger and mixed spice in a food processor. Add the butter and blend until the mixture looks like crumbs. Add the honey and process until it forms a soft dough. Remove this from the processor, wrap in clingfilm or greaseproof paper and chill for 30 minutes or until firm.

Lightly flour the work surface and a rolling pin, then roll out the dough to about 5 mm thick. Cut out shapes using cookie cutters. Use a cocktail stick to pierce a hole at the top of each one, large enough to thread a ribbon through.

Arrange the shapes on the prepared trays and chill for 10 minutes. Bake in a preheated oven at 180°C (350°F) Gas 4 for about 10 minutes until golden. Leave for 5 minutes, then transfer to a wire rack to cool. Decorate when cold.

Best eaten within 24 hours, or store in an airtight container and eat within 4 days. Undecorated cookies can be frozen for up to a month.

little indulgences

These 'kisses' are delicate little walnut and coffee biscuits joined with a rich chocolate-coffee ganache – a real treat!

walnut coffee kisses

100 g unsalted butter

70 g caster sugar

½ beaten egg

110 g self-raising flour

1 teaspoon instant espresso powder

40 g walnut halves, finely chopped

For the ganache:

100 g plain chocolate

40 g unsalted butter

125 ml double cream

1½ teaspoons instant espresso powder

several baking trays, lined with non-stick baking parchment

makes about 12

Put the butter and sugar into a bowl and beat until creamy. Stir in the beaten egg and then fold in the sifted flour. Stir in the espresso powder, then the walnuts.

Put an even number (about 24) tablespoons of the mixture onto baking trays covered with non-stick parchment. Bake in a preheated oven at 180°C (350°F) Gas 4 for about 10 minutes or until light-brown around the edges. Remove from the oven and let cool and firm up on the tray for a couple of minutes, then carefully transfer to a wire rack to cool completely.

Meanwhile, to make the ganache, break the chocolate into pieces and put into a small saucepan. Heat with butter and cream without boiling, until the butter melts. Beat in the espresso powder. Remove from the heat and stir. The mixture will thicken as it cools. Carefully sandwich the cool, fragile biscuits together with the ganache.

Store in an airtight container and eat within 24 hours.

What a combination! The two most popular sweet things sandwiched together. If you really do run out of time and can't make the cookies yourself then by all means buy them, but they will not be as good as this recipe.

chocolate chip cookie ice cream cakes

375 g unsalted butter

375 g golden caster sugar

3 eggs

1 teaspoon real vanilla essence

375 g plain flour

375 g dark chocolate, chopped

2.5 litres good ice cream

several baking trays, lined with non-stick baking parchment

makes about 24

Put the butter and sugar into a bowl and beat until light and fluffy. Add the eggs and vanilla and beat well. Add the flour and chocolate and fold until smooth. Working in batches, spoon out 48 portions of the mixture (2 teaspoons each) onto the prepared baking trays, making sure each biscuit has enough room to spread (they will triple in size). Bake in the middle of a preheated oven at 180°C (350°F) Gas 4 for about 15 minutes until lightly golden. Remove from the oven and let cool on the baking trays for 5 minutes. Transfer to a wire cooling rack and let cool completely.

Sandwich 2 biscuits together with ice cream, arrange on a tray, cover well with foil and return to the freezer until needed.

Transfer to the refrigerator 20-30 minutes before serving so that the ice cream can soften a little.

This is one for the kids. S'mores are an American campfire classic where biscuits, barbecued marshmallows and chocolate squares are sandwiched together making a deliciously gooey taste sensation. Although traditionally made with wholewheat crackers any sweet biscuit, such as *langue du chat* or almond thins, will work just as well.

s'mores

16 cookies of your choice (either homemade or shop bought)

8 squares of plain or milk chocolate

16 pink or white marshmallows

8 metal skewers

a barbecue

makes 4

Put 8 of the cookies onto a plate and top each one with a square of the chocolate.

Preheat the barbecue. Thread 2 marshmallows onto each skewer and cook over hot coals for about 2 minutes, turning constantly until the marshmallows are melted and blackened. Remove from the heat and let cool slightly.

Put the marshmallows on top of the chocolate squares and sandwich together with the remaining cookies.

Gently ease out the skewers and eat the s'mores as soon as the chocolate melts.

Though Austrian bakers are credited with inventing these cookies, their name implies an Italian heritage. The chewy, candylike florentine has a flat side which is coated with chocolate, then combed to give an attactive wavy pattern or feathered (dragged) design.

tiny florentines

85 g unsalted butter

85 g golden syrup

30 g plain flour

60 g chopped almonds

30 g chopped mixed peel

60 g sultanas or crystallized fruits

60 g glacé cherries, chopped

110 g chocolate – plain or white – or some of each, melted

several baking trays, lined with non-stick baking parchment

makes about 20

Put the butter and golden syrup into a medium, heavy-based saucepan and heat until melted. Stir in all the remaining ingredients except the chocolate.

Put teaspoonfuls of the mixture onto the prepared baking trays, spacing them well apart. Flatten lightly, then bake in a preheated oven at 180°C (350°F) Gas 4 for 7–8 minutes until light golden brown. Remove from the oven and let cool for 1–2 minutes or until firm enough to transfer to a wire rack to cool completely.

When cool, coat the flat underside of each florentine with the melted chocolate and, using a serrated icing spatula or small fork, make a wavy pattern in the chocolate. Leave to set, chocolate side up.

Store in a cool place in an airtight container. Best eaten within a week.

Use good-quality cookies, made with butter if possible – and of course, plenty of real chocolate chips. Inferior cookies will spoil the ice cream by giving it a greasy aftertaste when frozen.

chocolate chip cookie ice cream

250 g mascarpone cheese

250 ml whole milk

100 g light muscovado sugar

150 g chocolate chip cookies, crumbled

an ice cream machine (optional)

serves 4–6

Put the mascarpone, milk and sugar in a bowl and beat until smooth. Transfer the mixture to an ice cream machine and churn until almost frozen. Fold in the crumbled cookies and continue churning until the mixture is completely frozen. Transfer to a freezerproof container and freeze until ready to serve.

If you are making the ice cream without a machine, first freeze the mixture in a shallow container. When almost solid, beat it well with a wire whisk or electric beater until smooth, then return to the freezer. Repeat the process twice more to break down the ice crystals, folding in the crumbled cookies before returning it to the freezer for the final time. The result will be a smooth, silky ice cream.

Transfer to the refrigerator for 20–30 minutes to soften before serving. Best eaten within a week of being made.

Recipes

Linda Collister: pages 10, 13, 14, 17, 18, 21, 24, 27, 28, 31, 32, 35, 36, 38, 40, 43, 44, 48, 59

Hattie Ellis: page 52

Clare Ferguson: page 47

Liz Franklin: page 60

Louise Pickford: page 56

Fran Warde: page 55

Photographs

Key: tr=top right, br=bottom right, tl=top left, bl=bottom left

Diana Miller: pages 1, 2, 4–5, 6, 8 *tl, tr & bl*, 11, 12, 15, 19, 20, 22 *tl & br*, 26, 29, 30, 37, 38 *tl, tr & bl*, 41, 42, 45, 49, 62

Martin Brigdale: pages 22 *tr*, 25, 34, 38 *br*, 46, 50 *tr*, 58

Patrice de Villiers: pages 8 *br*, 16, 22 *bl*, 33

Debi Treloar: pages 50 *bl*, 53, 54

William Lingwood: page 50 *br*, 61

Ian Wallace: page 50 *tl*, 57